LETTS POCKET GUIDE TO

BUTTERFLIES

The most common species of
European butterflies
described and illustrated in colour

Pamela Forey and Sue McCormick

595'789 F63,540 .

CHARLES LETTS
Letts
of London®
FOUNDED 1796

Front cover illustration: Peacock

This edition first published in 1993
by Charles Letts & Co Ltd
Letts of London House
Parkgate Road
London SW11 4NQ

'Letts' is a registered trademark of
Charles Letts & Co Limited

This edition produced under licence by
Malcolm Saunders Publishing Ltd, London

© 1993 this edition Atlantis Publications Ltd

A CIP catalogue record for this book is available
from the British Library

ISBN 1 85238 393 3

Printed in Spain by Graficas Reunidas

Contents

Introduction

There are about 400 butterfly species in Europe, about 60 of them resident in the British Isles. We cannot include all of them in a book this size but we have selected the most common and widely distributed species for inclusion and designed the book for people who know little about butterflies. The book is simple to use and enables you to identify a butterfly you might see in your garden or on a walk; and gives you some information about it.

How to use this book

We have divided the book into sections based on the families of butterflies, since these are relatively clearcut and easy to distinguish from each other. With very little experience you will begin to spot the various families, and then identifying individual species becomes easier. The families are **Swallowtails & Apollos**; **Whites & Yellows**; **Blues**, **Coppers & Hairstreaks**; **Metalmarks**; **Aristocrats & Fritillaries**; **Browns**; **Milkweed Butterflies**; **Nettle-tree Butterflies**; **Skippers**. If you are already confident you can identify a butterfly as to its family, then you can turn directly to that section, in order to identify it more accurately. If however, you are unsure of the family to which it belongs, then you can use the key in the *Guide to Identification* which follows, to find the right family.

Guide to Identification

Butterflies are insects. Like all insects they have bodies with hard but flexible exoskeletons divided into three sections (head, thorax and abdomen); there are two antennae on the head; and three pairs of legs and two pairs of wings on the thorax.

Butterflies and moths can be distinguished from other insects by their scale-covered wings. And butterflies can be distinguished from moths by their antennae — butterfly antennae are knobbed or clubbed while moth antennae are variable in form but never have knobs or clubs. In general butterflies are brightly coloured, day-flying insects while moths are dull-coloured, night-flying insects (although there are exceptions to this rule); moths hold their wings flat over the body or in a roof-like position when at rest while butterflies hold their wings vertically. Skippers, although usually considered to be butterflies (they have clubbed antennae), are rather different to the rest, especially in the way they hold their wings.

In this guide we have used differences in the wing colours, antennae and legs to distinguish the butterflies of the various families. Details are also given for eggs, caterpillars and pupae (see also p. 15). Page numbers will enable you to turn directly to the relevant family.

Swallowtails and Apollos (family *Papilionidae*)

Large butterflies with brightly coloured wings, many (but not all) with a tail on each hind wing. All three pairs of legs fully developed; each leg ends in a single claw. Knob of antennae usually curved. Swallowtails have strong gliding flight, apollos and festoons flutter and flap.

Eggs hemispherical. Caterpillars variable but generally stout with only minute hairs when fully grown. A forked retractable gland just behind the head of the caterpillar can be extruded if it is threatened and produces an offensive scent. Pupae of swallowtails are formed without cocoons and suspended from a pad of silk by a silken girdle; pupae of festoons are attached to a stem by a silken thread at the head, and by the tail; pupae of apollos lie on the ground (often under stones) in loose cocoons.

11 species in Europe, 1 in the British Isles   **16–18**

Whites and Yellows (family *Pieridae*)

Medium-sized butterflies with white or yellow wings, often with black veins. (Wing colours come from waste products stored in the wings). All three pairs of legs fully developed; each leg ends in four claws. Males and females often different; spring and summer generations also often different. Knob of antenna straight. Many have a fluttery kind of flight but can nevertheless travel long distances. Several are famous migrants.

Eggs tall, bottle-shaped and ribbed. Caterpillars elongated and cylindrical, often green, with a covering of short hairs and no warts or spines. Pupae are formed without a cocoon but suspended upright from a pad of silk by a silken girdle; the tail end is attached to the silk pad and the head is pointed.

About 40 species in Europe, 6 resident in the British Isles   **19–29**

Blues, Hairstreaks and Coppers (family *Lycaenidae*)

Small often brightly coloured, metallic butterflies, males very different in colour from females. Males often blue or copper-coloured, females brown. However both sexes in any one species have similar markings on the undersides of the wings. First two pairs of legs in male slightly smaller than other legs, with only one claw each, otherwise legs fully developed with a pair of claws on each. Antennae have long clubs. Flight rapid but these butterflies do not travel far and often live in local colonies.

Eggs broader than high and disc-like, with rounded edges and a sculptured surface. Caterpillars shaped like woodlice, short and stout with a retractable head, and covered with short hairs. Many have a special gland on the back which produces honey dew. Pupae are also short and stout, formed without a cocoon. They may be attached to a leaf by the tail and with a silken girdle or lie loose among leaves on the ground.

About 100 species in Europe, 16 in the British Isles   **30–59**

Metalmarks (family *Riodinidae*)

Most closely related to the Blues, hairstreaks and coppers and sharing many features with members of that family. However males have only two pairs of functional walking legs, the first pair are much reduced and useless for walking; in the female all three pairs are fully developed.

Eggs small and spherical. Caterpillars short and stout like those of blues, but lack the honey dew gland. Pupae are also stout, formed without a cocoon and attached to plants by the tail and by a silken girdle.

1 species in Europe including the British Isles (the Duke of Burgundy Fritillary). **60**

Fritillaries and Aristocrats (family *Nymphalidae*)

Medium-sized to large, brightly coloured and brilliantly marked butterflies, males and females generally similar. First two legs small and held close under the head, so that the butterfly appears to have only four legs; in males the front legs are brush-like with long hair-scales, in females the legs have short hairs. Middle and hind two pairs of legs are fully developed and used for walking. Knob of antenna large, oval and flattened. These butterflies have a powerful flight and some travel long distances; others live in local colonies.

Eggs strongly ribbed, often conical or oval. Caterpillars cylindrical and usually spiny; those that lack spines often have horns behind the head. Pupae are also spiny and formed without a cocoon, suspended only by their tails from silken pads; they do not have a silken girdle.

About 70 species in Europe, 18 in Britain **61–88**

Browns (family *Satyridae*)

Mostly medium-sized butterflies, almost all (with the exception of Marbled Whites) some shade of brown, often with orange markings and/or eyespots on the wings. One or two veins in the fore wings are swollen at the base. Males and females usually different, although not strikingly so, and males have sex-brands on the fore wings. First two legs similar to those of aristocrats and fritillaries. Middle and hind two pairs of legs are fully developed and used for walking. Knobs of antennae vary from species to species. Flight often erratic and dancing, just over the top of the vegetation or ground; these butterflies do not travel long distances.

Eggs often barrel-shaped and ribbed. Caterpillars covered in short downy hairs and spindle-shaped, tapering to a relatively small head and to the tail; the tail is forked into two points. Pupae do not have a cocoon, and either lie unattached on the ground or are suspended from a plant by the tail; they do not have a silken girdle.

About 120 species in Europe, 11 in the British Isles **89–108**

Milkweed Butterflies (family *Danaidae*)

There are no naturally occurring members of this family in Europe, but the Monarch (page 109) has become naturalized in the Canary Islands and is found as an irregular migrant further north in Europe and in the British Isles. It is a large tawny orange butterfly, with the first pair of legs like that of aristocrats and fritillaries.

Monarch eggs are conical and ribbed. Caterpillar is transversely striped in green, black and yellow. Pupa is stumpy, pale green and suspended by a black thread. **109**

Fig. 1 Types of Butterflies

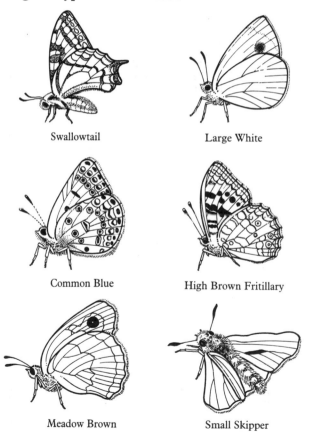

Swallowtail

Large White

Common Blue

High Brown Fritillary

Meadow Brown

Small Skipper

Nettle-tree Butterflies (family *Libytheidae*)

Small brown and orange butterflies with characteristic long palps which project from the front of the head like a snout. Fore wings have truncated tips and margins of hind wings are scalloped. In the male, the first pair of legs is reduced like those of aristocrats and fritillaries, and only the middle and hind legs are used for walking; in females all three pairs of legs are fully developed.

Eggs oval and ridged. Caterpillars cylindrical, slightly hairy, green or brown in colour. Pupae are stout, angular and ridged, formed without a cocoon and suspended by the tail only.

One species in Europe, none in the British Isles   **110**

Skippers (family *Hesperiidae*)

Small orange brown to dark grey butterflies with wings different in structure from all other butterflies, in that all the veins arise from the cells and do not branch. Males have sex brands on the fore wings. Skippers have thick moth-like bodies; their broad heads are usually wider than the thorax and bear large, protruding eyes. Antennae have widely separated bases and end in tapering clubs, often pointed and more or less hooked at the tip. All three pairs of legs are fully developed and used for walking; the hind legs in many species bear spurs (like many moths). Flight is rapid and darting, and skippers are often described as skipping from flower to flower.

Eggs variable; they have no form which is characteristic of the family. Caterpillar has a broad head separated from the rest of the body by a constricted 'neck' (actually the constricted first segment); the body tapers at both ends and is sparsely hairy. Caterpillar lives in a shelter formed from leaves or grasses, linked together by silk. Pupae are formed in their leafy shelters, inside silken cocoons.

About 40 species in Europe, 8 in the British Isles   **111–121**

Making a positive identification

In the box at the top of each page you will find the Common and Latin names of the butterfly together with its size, given in the size symbol (see Fig. 2) and as an actual measurement of the wingspan (measured from the centre of the thorax along each wing to its tip, not from tip to tip). At the foot of each page is the time of year at which the butterfly is likely to be seen. Latitude and elevation are critical factors influencing the emergence of butterflies from their pupae, and where a species flies at different times in the northern and southern parts of its range, this has been indicated. Where a butterfly flies in both mountain and lowland areas it usually emerges earlier in the season in the lowlands than in the mountains.

Fig. 2 Key to size symbols

  Less than 30mm

  30–55mm

55–70mm

70–100mm

On each page, four boxes of text provide details which make positive identification possible. The first box gives information on colour and wing patterns which, together with the illustration, enable you to identify your butterfly. Details of habitat and distribution are given in the second box (and the distribution is also given in the map in the illustration). The third box gives you information on the caterpillar and its foodplant. Finally the fourth box indicates some species with which it might be confused and/or gives some idea of the variation within the species. Those species printed in **Bold** are illustrated, either as featured species or in the *Other Common Species* sections; those printed in ordinary type are not.

Fig. 3 Distribution Map

●   Widespread and resident in this area

○   Partial distribution only or reaching the limits of its distribution in this area

*   Migrates into this area during the summer

Other Common Species

At the end of certain groups of butterflies (*Blues* and *Browns* for instance) you will find pages of *Other Common Species*. These are mostly less widespread than the featured butterflies, less likely to be encountered or very similar to one of the featured species.

Now you are ready to use this book. It is designed to fit into your pocket, so take it with you on your next outing and don't forget to tick your sightings on the checklist provided with the index. Butterflies are among the most beautiful living things in the world, far more beautiful alive and in flight than in a box. Many are endangered by development or changes in land practice, like many other animal and plant species and some are protected species. So please do not collect them but take a photograph instead.

Life History of a Butterfly

Butterflies, like many other insects, have a complicated life cycle. Males search for females by sight and then court them. Many males produce a pleasant scent from special scales on their fore wings (the scales are often but not always gathered into sex brands), and he scatters this scent around the female as he courts her. After mating, the females lay their eggs on a wide variety of plants, sometimes singly, sometimes in rows or clusters, usually on the undersides of leaves.

The larvae or caterpillars emerge after a few days or may remain in the eggs over the winter to emerge in spring. The caterpillar, as illustrated in the diagram, is quite different to the adult butterfly in form and lifestyle. At first the caterpillar is very small but it grows quickly, feeding on the leaves or flowers of the foodplant on which the eggs were laid. It sheds its skin several times during this period and its appearance may change considerably after each skin

Fig. 4 Specimen Page

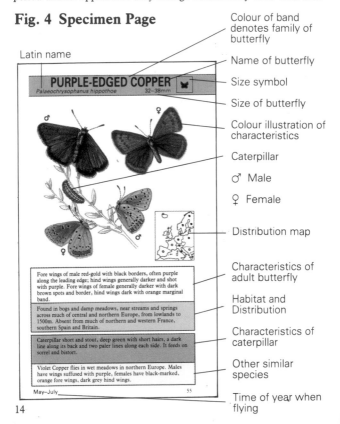

Colour of band denotes family of butterfly

Latin name

PURPLE-EDGED COPPER
Palaeochrysophanus hippothoe   32–38mm

Name of butterfly

Size symbol

Size of butterfly

Colour illustration of characteristics

Caterpillar

♂ Male

♀ Female

Distribution map

Fore wings of male red-gold with black borders, often purple along the leading edge; hind wings generally darker and shot with purple. Fore wings of female generally darker with dark brown spots and border, hind wings dark with orange marginal band.

Characteristics of adult butterfly

Found in bogs and damp meadows, near streams and springs across much of central and northern Europe, from lowlands to 1500m. Absent from much of northern and western France, southern Spain and Britain.

Habitat and Distribution

Caterpillar short and stout, deep green with short hairs, a dark line along its back and two paler lines along each side. It feeds on sorrel and bistort.

Characteristics of caterpillar

Violet Copper flies in wet meadows in northern Europe. Males have wings suffused with purple, females have black-marked, orange fore wings, dark grey hind wings.

Other similar species

May–July   55

Time of year when flying

14

change. The descriptions given in the texts refer to the fully grown caterpillar.

Once it reaches its full size it becomes lethargic. At this stage some caterpillars spin a cocoon of silk, but all find a hiding place unique to the species and shed their skin for a final time. The form that emerges is quite different (see Fig. 5) and is called a pupa or chrysalis. Its skin soon hardens and inside radical changes take place in the form of the animal, a process called metamorphosis. At the end of this process the pupa splits open and the adult butterfly emerges.

The adult butterfly has a 'furry' body divided into three parts, the head, thorax and abdomen. Attached to the thorax are two pairs of brightly coloured, scale-covered wings (two fore wings and two hind wings), and three pairs of legs. In its mouth the butterfly has a long, coiled, tubular proboscis which it uses to feed on the nectar of flowers; there are furry palps in front of the proboscis and long club-bed antennae on the top of the head.

Fig. 5 Life Cycle of a Butterfly

SWALLOWTAIL
64–100mm

Papilio machaon

Wings yellow with dense black markings; broad black border with yellow spots on back of fore wings. Broad black border on back of hind wings contains blurred blue spots and yellow crescents. Hind wings tailed, with single red spot at base.

Found in meadows and flowery grassy places, from lowlands to mountains (up to about 2000m). Throughout continental Europe but becoming more rare than formerly in the central countries. Confined to the Norfolk Broads in Britain. Protected.

Caterpillar green, striped with black and orange. It protrudes a pair of orange horns if startled. Feeds mainly on umbelliferous plants like milk parsley, wild carrot and fennel.

Southern Festoon flies in lowland meadows of southern Europe, Spanish Festoon in hills and mountains. Both have yellow wings with black bands, red spots and zigzag-like black borders.

April–May & July–Aug (S); May–July (N & GB)

SCARCE SWALLOWTAIL

Iphiclides podalirius   65–90mm

Wings pale creamy yellow, with six dark vertical stripes on each fore wing. Hind wings have a black border along the rear edges, studded with blue crescent-shaped spots and with a single red crescent above innermost blue spot. Hind wings have long tails.

Found in gardens and hedges, woods and orchards in lowland areas of Europe, from the Mediterranean to Belgium and Germany. Occasional vagrants reach the North and Baltic Seas or cross the Channel into southern England. Protected.

Caterpillar green with a yellow stripe along the back and oblique yellow side stripes. Feeds on hawthorn, sloe, cherries and other fruit trees.

Southern Swallowtail has bright yellow wings and four stripes on fore wings; it is found in foothills of Alps, especially on western slopes.

April–June & Aug–Sept   17

Wings of male white, of female greyish. Both sexes have two large black spots and several smaller ones in the fore wings; hind wings have two black-bordered, red spots, often with white centres to the spots. Other spots may also be present.

Found in mountains from southern Spain, Sicily and Turkey to Scandinavia, at altitudes of 700–1800m in the south, lower in the north. Most often in valleys and meadows. Absent from Britain. Rare in some areas of central Europe. Protected.

Caterpillar velvety black with short black hairs growing from raised warts, and red spots along the sides. Feeds on various species of stonecrops and houseleeks.

Clouded Apollo flies in mountain meadows in central Europe; it has no red spots, only two black spots on fore wings. Small Apollo (with many red spots) is confined to the Alps.

BLACK-VEINED WHITE

Aporia crataegi   55–68mm

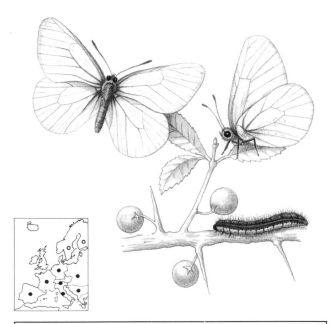

Wings white. Males have dark brown or black veins and some black scales on the undersides of the wings. Females larger, with brown veins and few scales on the wings so that they look almost transparent.

Found in open woodland and clearings, orchards and open country from sea level to 1800m, throughout continental Europe, north to central Scandinavia and Finland. The species became extinct in Britain in the 1920s.

Caterpillar malodorous, with poisonous hairs, brownish or grey with wide black band on back and two rusty side-stripes. Feeds in groups in silken webs, on hawthorn, plum, blackthorn and other *Prunus* species and at one time were pests in orchards.

Clouded Apollo has black spots on wings. Dark-veined White is a form of the **Green-veined White** found in the mountains; males have black veins on the upper sides of the wings.

May–July   19

Wings white or yellowish with black tips and a black mark on front edge of hind wing. Undersides of hind wings and tips of fore wings yellow or grey. Females have two black spots and a black streak on fore wing; males have no spots on upper side but two black spots on underside of fore wing.

Common in gardens, found in many other places, from lowlands to 1800m throughout Europe and the British Isles, north to central Scandinavia and Finland. Many individuals migrate long distances.

Caterpillars are notorious pests on cabbages and other brassicas, feeding in groups and making large holes in the leaves. They are grey-green with yellow and black markings and short white hairs. They smell unpleasant.

Small White is smaller and has much smaller, less well defined markings.

20   April–May & July–Aug, also Sept–Oct

Artogeia rapae   45–55mm

F 63,540

Wings white or yellowish with dark tips; underside of fore wings white with a yellow tip and two black spots on each, of hind wings yellow. Male has one small grey or black spot on fore wing, female has two small spots and a dash.

Found in gardens, meadows, roadsides and many other places, from sea level to 1800m, throughout the British Isles and Europe, north to central Scandinavia and Finland. One of the most common butterflies. Many migrate long distances.

Caterpillars are pests on cabbages and other brassicas, feeding singly on many cruciferous plants in the wild. They are greenish with a yellow stripe along the back, a row of yellow spots along the sides and many white hairs.

Two other small whites, Southern Small White and Mountain Small White, fly in rough rocky places in southern Europe. **Large White** is much larger, with larger spots.

Mar–May & June–Sept/Oct   21

GREEN-VEINED WHITE
35–50mm   *Artogeia napi*

Undersides of hind wings yellow, with veins picked out in grey or greenish scales. Some summer forms lack this veining. Upper sides of wings white or yellowish with grey or black veins and a dark tip, one black spot on fore wings in males, at least two in females.

Found in open countryside, often near water, in damp meadows and open woodland, along woodland margins, from marshland to mountain valleys, from sea level to over 2500m. Throughout Europe and the British Isles.

Caterpillar green with yellow rings around the spiracles, and covered with short white hairs. Feeds on wild crucifers, charlock, watercress etc, but rarely on garden brassicas.

Dark-veined White is a form that occurs in the mountains; males have black veins on the upper sides of the wings. **Large White** has yellow underside to the hind wings, without the grey veins.

Fore wings creamy white with patchy black and white tips and a central black spot; hind wings white. Undersides of hind wings and tips of fore wings dappled with green markings, dense green in spring brood, paler and yellow-green in summer brood.

Found in open meadows and on hillsides to 1400m in southern Europe, from Portugal and Spain, through southern France and Italy, to the Balkans and Turkey.

Caterpillar pale blue-green with black spots; a dark grey-green, yellow-edged stripe runs along the back; a white stripe runs along each side, bordered with yellow on its lower side. Feeds on cruciferous plants, like candytuft and wild radish.

Several similar species occur in southern Europe, like Mountain Dappled White, found high in Alps and Pyrenees. Hind wing of **Bath White** has one black spot in male, many in female.

Fore wings white with dappled black tips and a central black spot, females more heavily marked than males. Hind wings mainly white in males, with black markings in females. Undersides of hind wings and tips of fore wings mainly green with white spots.

Found in meadows, fields and rough ground in central and southern Europe, north to France and Germany. Many individuals migrate long distances, occasional vagrants fly further north and to England, rarely Norway and Ireland.

Caterpillar grey-mauve with two yellow stripes on each side, yellow spots above prolegs, many black spots and white hairs. Feeds on mignonettes and cruciferous plants, especially mustards.

Undersides of hind wings and fore wing tips mainly olive green in spring brood, yellow-green in summer brood. **Dappled White** is confined to southern Europe and has white hind wings.

Feb–Mar, April–May & July–Aug

Wings white, fore wings with a dark grey or black tip and a single black spot. In males this spot is just inside a wide apical band of orange. Undersides of hind wings dappled with yellow-green markings.

Found in meadows, around hedgerows and woodland edges, along woodland tracks, up to 1500m. Throughout most of the British Isles (less common in Scotland) and Europe, north to northern Sweden and Finland.

Caterpillar green along the back, shading into blue-green on the sides, dark green beneath, with many black or white bristles. Feeds on cruciferous plants, mainly on ripening seed pods, of plants like garlic mustard and cuckoo flower.

Morocco Orange Tip flies in mountains of Spain and Portugal; it has yellow wings. Female Orange Tip is similar to **Dappled White**; both have dappled green undersides to the hind wings.

April–June   25

WOOD WHITE
35–48mm

Leptidea sinapis

A small butterfly with creamy white wings. Tips of fore wings are grey in spring brood, grey in females and black in males in summer brood. Undersides of wings also creamy white, suffused with yellow-grey on hind wings and parts of fore wings.

Found in glades and rides in open woodland, throughout much of Europe, north to northern Scandinavia and Finland. Also from central and southern England to south Wales and Ireland. Recognizable from its weak fluttering flight.

Caterpillar green with a dark line along the back and a yellow stripe on each side. Feeds on members of the pea family including bird's-foot trefoil, meadow vetchling and vetches.

Two similar wood whites occur in Europe. Eastern Wood White flies in Alps and mountains of southeastern Europe. Fenton's Wood White flies in lowland areas of central eastern Europe.

26

May–June & July–Aug (S)

Fore wings hooked, hind wings with blunt tails. Males have sulphur-yellow wings, females greenish white wings; both have an orange spot on each wing.

Found in open places and woodland, wandering all over Europe, the southern half of Britain and all Ireland. They live for up to a year, hatching in summer and flying until autumn, then hibernating. Spring butterflies have emerged from hibernation.

Caterpillar blue-green with black speckles on its back, with a white stripe along each side, and yellow-green beneath. Feeds on leaves of buckthorn.

The Cleopatra is a very similar butterfly found in Mediterranean Europe; however the hind wing tails may be almost non-existent and the males have orange fore wings.

Apr–May & June–Sept

27

CLOUDED YELLOW

46–54mm

Colias crocea

Wings bright orange-yellow with black borders, and one round black spot on each fore wing. Undersides have dark spots on fore wing and a silver spot on hind wing. In females the black borders contain yellow spots; some females have pale creamy wings.

A famous migrant butterfly. Resident in central and southern Europe, in open places and heaths to 1800m, but migrating to northern Europe and Britain, in occasional years in thousands. In a bad year only a few individuals migrate north.

Caterpillar velvety green with many black spots, each with a single white hair. Yellowish line with orange-red dashes runs along each side. Feeds on members of the pea family, especially on clovers and lucerne, but also on bird's-foot trefoil.

One of over 10 Clouded Yellows in Europe. Most males have paler wings, e.g. sulphur-coloured Moorland Clouded Yellow, found in moors and bogs in N. Europe. Females often white.

April–May & July–Oct

♂

♀

Wings of male pale yellow, of female white tinted with yellow-green. Both have black, white-blotched borders and red fringes, an oval black spot on the fore wing and an orange spot on the hind wing.

Another famous migrant. Resident, common in some years and scarce in others, in central Europe north of the Pyrenees, in meadows, lucerne and clover fields to over 1800m. They migrate north, in large numbers in some years, occasionally to Britain.

Caterpillar velvety green with an orange and yellow-white stripe along each side, and many short black hairs. Feeds on lucerne, vetches and other plants in the pea family.

Berger's Clouded Yellows often fly with Pale Clouded Yellows. Their females are difficult to distinguish but male Bergers have brighter yellow wings with less extensive black markings.

May–June & Aug–Sept   29

Wings of male violet blue and hairy with a narrow dark border; of female brown towards the edges, blue in the centre. Both sexes have tailed hind wings. Undersides beige with transverse creamy stripes, on the hind wing one stripe wider than the others. There are dark spots near the tail.

Found in rough places, flowery meadows and fields, from lowlands to 2000m. Resident in southern Europe but migrating north each year, reaching France, Belgium and Germany by late summer, occasionally crossing the Channel to southern England.

Caterpillar short and stout, varying in colour from dark green to reddish brown, with a dark stripe along the back and oblique stripes on the sides. It feeds on pods of various leguminous plants, especially bladder senna but also peas.

Lang's Short-tailed Blue is smaller and has a beige and white striped pattern on the undersides without one stripe larger than others. Found in lowland grassland in southern Europe.

May–Sept

Wings of male violet blue with a narrow dark border; of female dark brown, slightly suffused with blue. Both sexes have tailed hind wings; undersides of wings pale grey with lines of small black spots and orange spots near the edge of the hind wing.

Found in rough lowland grassland, meadows and heaths, often in damp places. Central and southern Europe from the Pyrenees to northern France and east to Greece; occasionally found further north and in Britain. Absent central and S. Spain.

Caterpillar short and stout, pale green with a darker stripe along the back and pale oblique stripes along the sides. It feeds on pods and leaves of leguminous plants, including medicks, bird's-foot trefoil and gorse.

Provençal Short-tailed Blue is similar but has no orange spots; it is scattered through southern Europe. **Small Blue** and **Silver-studded Blue** lack tails.

April–Sept

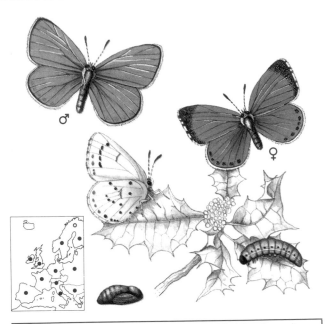

Wings of male sky blue, with a very narrow black border on fore wings. Wings of female darker blue with broad black borders on wings and six black spots on each hind wing. Undersides of both sexes pale blue-white with lines of black spots.

Found in open woodland, gardens and parks, females around holly or ivy, throughout much of Europe except north-west Scandinavia, in England, Wales and Ireland, most commonly in the south.

Caterpillar resembles a woodlouse with a hump, and is green, most often with an indefinite yellow stripe along the sides, but sometimes with maroon or rose-pink stripes. Feeds on holly and ivy, usually spring brood on holly and summer brood on ivy.

Small Blue has similar underside but is much smaller, with dark upper surface to its wings. Female may be mistaken for **Large Blue** but this has darker grey or grey-brown underside.

GREEN-UNDERSIDE BLUE

Glaucopsyche alexis

26–36mm

Wings of male purple-blue with narrow black borders, of females brown suffused with blue. Undersides pale grey flushed with green on the hind wings, and a line of large white-ringed black spots on the fore wings. There may be a few small spots on the hind wings.

Found around woodland edges or dry meadows, in hills and mountains up to 1200m. Western and northern Europe, from northern Spain to southern Scandinavia and Finland, more common in the south. Absent Britain, N. Germany and Denmark.

Caterpillar short and stout, shaggy, green or brown with a red-brown line along its back and red-brown oblique stripes on its sides. It feeds on various leguminous plants, including milk vetches and broom.

Black-eyed Blue is similar; it is found around broom plants in Spain. **Large Blue** has many black spots on the underside and a line of black spots on the upper surface of its fore wings.

April–June

Wings of male pale dull blue with narrow black borders, of female grey-brown, sometimes flushed with blue at wing bases and/or with indistinct spots. Undersides light brown with lines of white-ringed, black spots.

Found in marshy places and damp meadows from lowlands to 900m, locally in central Europe from France eastwards, south to the Alps and northern Spain, north to Germany and southern Sweden. Absent in Britain.

Caterpillar green or reddish brown. Young caterpillars feed on gentian flowers but after the third moult they are carried into ants' nests by the ants and complete their development in the nest, overwintering there and pupating in the spring.

A mountain form flies in alpine meadows and slopes up to 1800m, in the Pyrenees and Alps for instance. Its wings are brighter blue and slightly flushed with green on the underside.

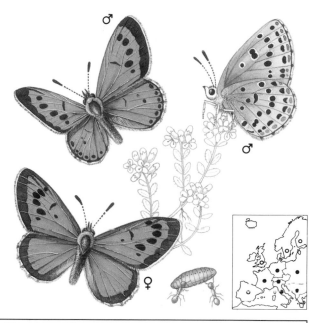

Wings bright blue with broad black borders and a series of long black spots on each fore wing; spots larger in female than male. Underside grey to grey-brown, flushed with iridescent green at base of hind wings, and with lines of white-ringed black spots.

Found in rough grassy places up to 1800m where wild thyme and ants nests are present. Northern Spain to southern Sweden and east to the Balkans and Greece. Became extinct in Britain in 1979, now reintroduced in one or two places and protected.

Caterpillar short and stout, pale pink with white stripes at first, feeding on thyme flowers. Mature caterpillar falls to ground and produces honeydew; it becomes white and swollen and is taken by a *Myrmica* ant to its nest where it pupates.

Male **Alcon Blue** has no spots on upper sides of wings, female has wings suffused grey-brown. Much rarer Scarce Large Blue and Dusky Large Blue fly in wet meadows in central Europe.

SILVER-STUDDED BLUE
24–34mm   *Plebejus argus*

Wings of male bright mauve-blue with narrow dark brown borders; of female dark brown slightly flushed with blue and with orange crescents on both wings. Undersides of male grey, of female grey-brown; marginal orange crescents have blue-centred, dark spots to the outside.

Found in grassy places, heaths and downs, hills and mountains scattered throughout Europe north to northern Scandinavia. In Britain it is now mainly found in southern and eastern England and in western Wales.

Caterpillar short and stout, shaped like a woodlouse, green or brown, with a white-bordered, dark brown stripe along the back and a white stripe on each side. Feeds on gorse, heather or bird's-foot trefoil. Attended by ants.

Idas Blue is slightly larger and often has a band of orange on hind wings; it is absent from Britain and Iberia. **Common Blue** has no blue in the orange and black spots on the undersides.

May–August

IDAS BLUE

Lycaeides idas

28–34mm

Wings of male bright blue with narrow black border; of female brown, with brown crescents especially on hind wings, and often blue at the base. Undersides grey or yellow-grey with many black spots and blue-centred, orange marginal spots often forming a wide band.

Found in sandy heathland, rough places and mountain slopes up to 1500m, throughout most of Europe. Absent from southern Spain and Portugal and from Britain.

Caterpillar short and stout, green or brown with a dark red-brown, white-edged stripe along each flank and white stripes on its sides. At first it feeds on leguminous plants or buckthorn, but mature caterpillars are taken by ants to their nests to overwinter.

Silver-studded Blue is very similar but is generally smaller; its orange crescents have blue-centred black spots to the outside.

June–July

Wings of male blue with dusky brown margins; of female brown, often flushed with blue and with orange crescents on hind wings. Underside of male dove grey, of female grey-brown, both with white-ringed black spots and a row of black-edged orange spots.

Found in dry meadows and hillsides up to 1500m, local but widely distributed across southern Europe from northern Spain to Balkans and through eastern Europe to Scandinavia. Absent from northwest Europe, including Britain, France and Germany.

Caterpillar green with long pale hairs; it has a dark green, light-edged stripe on its back and a yellowish stripe on each side. Its head is hidden from above by the swollen front segments. It feeds on tufted vetch and is tended by ants.

Damon Blue has wide dusky margins to pale shining blue wings, and yellow grey undersides with a white streak in middle of hind wing. It flies in mountains in continental Europe.

Wings of male pale silver blue with narrow black border on fore wings, breaking into black spots on hind wings; of female dark brown with black-centred orange spots on hind wings.
Underside of male pale grey, of female brown, both with white-ringed black spots, the outer ones edged with orange crescents.

Found in chalk and limestone grassland from sea level to 1800m. Northern Spain to the Baltic coast in Germany and eastward to the Balkans. Also found in southern England. Absent from the rest of Britain and Denmark.

Caterpillar resembles a bright green woodlouse with a hump; it has yellow stripes on back and sides. It feeds at night on horseshoe vetch in Britain, on this and other small leguminous plants in Europe. Full-grown in June. Tended by ants.

Adonis Blue females are similar to Chalk-hill females but the orange crescents on their hind wings are edged with blue instead of white.

July–August

Wings of male vivid sky blue with fine black line on margins; of female dark brown with orange, blue and black spots on hind wings. Underside pale grey-brown in male, darker in female, with white-ringed black spots and a marginal row of orange spots edged with black and white.

Found in small colonies in open chalk downs with short turf. Southern and central Europe from Portugal and Spain to the Balkans and north to France and Poland, also in southern England but now rare. Absent from Scandinavia.

Caterpillar shaped like a woodlouse with a hump, dark green with yellow stripes along back and sides, very similar to that of Chalk-hill Blue but full-grown in April and July. Feeds by day on horseshoe vetch or other small legumes. Tended by ants.

Chalk-hill Blue females are similar but have no blue in the spots on their hind wings. **Common Blue** males have pale violet blue wings and darker undersides flushed with blue.

May–June & July–Sept

Wings of male pale violet-blue; of female brown, variably flushed with violet-blue, and with orange crescents edged with black. Underside of male grey-beige, of female brown, both flushed with blue, with white-ringed black spots and a row of marginal black spots edged with orange and white crescents.

Found in grassland, meadows and grassy dunes, roadside verges and waste places, in woodland clearings and heathland, from sea level to 2000m. Common throughout Europe and the British Isles.

Caterpillar short and stout with an arched back, dark green with a darker line along the back and a paler line along each side. It feeds on small leguminous plants, including bird's-foot trefoil, restharrow and white clover. Tended by ants.

Adonis Blue male has sky blue wings and paler grey undersides. Common Blue females with no blue on wings resemble **Brown Argus** females; with blue, they resemble **Adonis Blue** females.

April–Sept   41

BATON BLUE
20–25mm
Pseudophilotes baton

Wings of male powder blue with a narrow black border and a long black spot on each fore wing; of female dark brown flushed with blue at the base. Underside of both sexes pale grey to grey-brown with lines of prominent black spots and black-edged orange crescents along the margin of each hind wing.

Found in dry grassy places with thyme plants, up to 2000m but not common. Central Europe from northern Spain and Portugal north to northern France and east to Poland. Absent from Britain, Holland, much of Germany, Denmark and Scandinavia.

Caterpillar short, stout and warty in appearance, dark green with wine red and white stripes on back and sides and white hairs. First brood caterpillars feed on wild thyme, second brood feed on mint, savory and lavender. Tended by ants.

Panoptes Blue and False Baton Blue are related butterflies found in central and southern Spain; they have no orange crescents on the underside of the hind wings.

April–June & July–Sept

Very small butterflies with dark brown wings. Males have a covering of silver-blue scales on their wings, especially near the wing bases. Undersides pale grey, tinged with yellow in females, with lines of white-ringed, black spots in both sexes.

Found in chalk and limestone grassland, in quarries and woodland rides, on roadsides and cliffs, from sea level to 2000m. Northern Spain to the coasts of Scandinavia. Local in Britain and Ireland, mainly in southern England.

Caterpillar short and stout, like a woodlouse with a hump, pale yellow-brown with a whitish stripe along each side. It feeds only on kidney vetch in Britain, on this and other small leguminous plants in Europe.

Short-tailed Blue is similar on the underside and females are brown but its hind wings have short tails.

May–August

43

♂

Wings dark brown with a marginal row of orange crescents, larger in the female. Underside pale grey-brown with lines of white-ringed, dark brown spots, and a row of white spots towards the edge, each enclosing an orange crescent and a brown spot.

Found in chalk and limestone grassland, heathland, coastal cliffs and dunes, from sea level to 900m. Found throughout Europe north to southern Scandinavia and Britain (England and Wales).

Caterpillar shaped like a woodlouse, pale green with discontinuous purple stripes along back and sides. It feeds on rockrose, stork's-bill or dove's-foot cranesbill. Usually found in the company of ants.

May be confused with females of more typical blues. Northern Brown Argus flies in mountains in southern Europe (southern form), in moorland in the north and Scotland (northern form).

April–Sept

Wings dark brown, unmarked in male, with a few orange crescents on hind wings in female. Underside grey to grey-brown, flushed with blue at base of hind wing; with white-ringed black spots, a white streak in the middle and variable orange crescents on hind wings, larger on females.

Found in meadows, in hills and mountains up to 2400m, from northern Spain to the Balkans, and north through eastern Europe to eastern Scandinavia and Finland. Absent from NW. Europe, including Britain, France, Germany and Denmark.

Caterpillar green with a yellow stripe along its back, and white and yellow stripes on the sides. It has a black head covered with yellowish hairs. It feeds on crane's-bills.

Northern Brown Argus has well developed orange crescents on the upper sides of its wings; the northern form has a single white spot on each fore wing.

June–July   45

OTHER BLUES

Chequered Blue (1)
Wingspan: 22–28mm. Northern form (found in S. Scandinavia & Finland) has dull blue wings with grey margins & chequered black & white borders.
Southern form (found from N. Spain across C. & S. Europe to Greece) has very dark wings with little blue (male) or black wings (female). Underside of both forms white with large black spots & an orange band on margin of hind wing. Found in rough dry places. Flies June–July. Caterpillars feed on stonecrops.

Mazarine Blue (2)
Wingspan: 25–34mm. Wings of male dull violet-blue with black borders; of female brown. Underside of both sexes light brown flushed with blue, & with a line of white-ringed black spots. Found in lowland & mountain meadows up to 1800m. Widespread across Europe from N. Spain to Greece & north to Scandinavia; rare in S. Spain & Portugal, extinct in Britain. Flies June–Aug. Caterpillar feeds on thrift, kidney vetch & clovers.

Turquoise Blue (1)
Wingspan: 30–44mm. Wings of male brilliant pale blue with narrow black margins; of female brown with orange crescents on hind wings. Undersides pale grey with broad white margins & lines of white-ringed black spots. Found locally in mountain meadows & slopes from 900–1500m in mountain areas of S. & C. Europe from N. Spain to the Balkans. Flies May–July & Aug–Sept. Caterpillar feeds on melilot, kidney vetch, clover & thyme.

Meleager's Blue (2)
Wingspan: 30–38mm. Hind wings have scalloped margins. Wings brilliant blue with black margins, darker blue in female than male with wider margins. Underside of male pale grey, of female light brown, both with white-ringed black spots & grey markings around margin. Found on slopes of limestone hills & downs from lowlands to 1300m. NE. Spain & S. France, through hills & mountains of S. Europe eastwards. Flies June. Caterpillar feeds on sainfoin, milkvetch & other legumes.

BROWN HAIRSTREAK
34–36mm

Thecla betulae

♂

Wings brown with small tails on hind wings and orange-red patches on either side of the tails; females have a broad orange-red transverse band on fore wing. Undersides of wings orange-yellow with transverse darker orange band bordered by white stripes.

Found around hedgerows and woodland edges, males high in trees (often oak or ash), females around blackthorn bushes laying eggs. Throughout much of Europe, England and S. Ireland. Absent from Mediterranean area and much of Scandinavia.

Caterpillar short and stout, triangular in cross-section and covered in short hairs. It is bright green with yellow stripes and well camouflaged on the blackthorn it feeds on, hiding beneath the leaves by day, feeding by night.

Sloe and **Ilex Hairstreaks** have brown wings but the undersides of their wings are also brown, with red or orange spots on hind wings.

♂

Wings of males iridescent purple with black edges; of female purple-black with more or less V-shaped, iridescent purple mark at base of fore wing. Hind wings of both have small tails. Undersides grey, with dark brown and white lines near the edge and orange spots.

Seen flying around the tops of oak and ash trees in woodland, sometimes in large numbers; they are attracted to and feed on aphid honeydew. Found throughout much of the British Isles and Europe, north to S. Scotland and S. Scandinavia.

Caterpillar broad and flattened, reddish-brown with a dark stripe along the back and oblique stripes on the sides. It is found on oak trees, hiding in a nest of silk by day and feeding on young leaves by night.

Spanish Purple Hairstreaks fly around ash trees in mountains of France and Spain. They resemble Purple Hairstreaks but have wide yellow borders on the yellow-grey undersides of the wings.

July–Sept   49

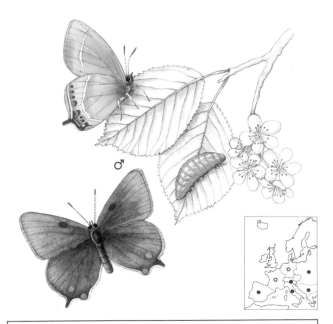

♂

Wings dark brown with small tails on hind wings and small orange spots near tails. Undersides of wings paler brown with white stripe across both wings, plus a blue spot near the tail and a row of orange spots on the hind wings.

Found in rough dry places from lowlands up to 1800m, often in hills, around shrubs of blackthorn and buckthorn. Common in central and southern Europe, north to northern Germany. Absent from the northwest, including NW. France and Britain.

Caterpillar short and stout, finely hairy, green with yellow-green diagonal stripes high on its sides and a yellow stripe along its back. It feeds on blackthorn or buckthorn.

No other Hairstreak has a blue spot near the tail on the underside of the hind wing.

Wings dark brown, slightly paler in females; hind wings have small tails. Undersides brown, with a white line on both wings, the line forming a W near the tail of the hind wings; and a line of orange, black-centred crescents on the hind wings.

Rarely seen as they rest high up in elm trees in hedgerows and woods. Their numbers were drastically reduced with the death of many elms from Dutch Elm disease, but they are still found throughout much of Europe and in southern England.

Caterpillar shaped like a humped woodlouse, yellow-green with oblique white stripes on the sides and a yellow stripe along the back, camouflaged to resemble the young elm leaves on which it feeds.

Black Hairstreak is found locally around blackthorn across much of Europe, in the Midlands in England. Male has orange spots on rear of fore wings, female has spots on both wings.

June–August

Wings dark brown with small tails on hind wings. Undersides paler brown with white line across both wings (often faint or broken on fore wings) and orange crescents on rear of hind wings. The crescents enclose black spots near the tail.

Found around blackthorn bushes in rough places. Across Europe, from northern Spain eastwards to Greece and the Balkans, north to central France and southern Germany.

Caterpillar short and stout, finely hairy, yellow-green with two yellow stripes along its back. It feeds on blackthorn.

Ilex Hairstreak flies around oaks. It is larger, the undersides of its wings are darker and its crescents are red, with black borders. Sometimes it has an orange blotch on the fore wings.

Wings dark brown, sometimes with an orange blotch on the fore wing. Hind wings have small tails. Undersides paler brown with irregular white line across both wings and red crescents on rear of hind wings. The crescents may have black borders with a white line on the inside.

Found around oaks on rough slopes from lowlands up to 1500m in the south. Southern and central Europe, north to southern Sweden and Finland, but more common in south and scarce in north. Absent from southern Spain and Britain.

Caterpillar short and stout, light green with a black head, a black, light-edged line along its back and oblique dark stripes on the sides. It feeds on the leaves of various oak trees.

Sloe Hairstreak is smaller, the undersides of its wings are paler and its crescents orange; it never has an orange blotch on fore wings. It flies around blackthorn.

June–July   53

Wings brown, with scalloped edges to hind wings. Undersides metallic green with faint or broken line of white spots across hind wings. Face of butterfly and borders around the eyes are green.

Found in rough ground, in woodland clearings and margins, on heaths, downs and hillsides up to 2000m, males perching on shrubs, females around brambles, gorse and other plants. Throughout Europe and the British Isles.

Caterpillar shaped like a woodlouse, bright green with conspicuous oblique yellow stripes on the sides. It feeds on young shoots of a wide variety of plants, including gorse, broom, bird's-foot trefoil, bilberry, buckthorn and dogwood.

Chapman's Green Hairstreak is found only in Spain and southern France, near Strawberry Trees. It is very similar to the Green Hairstreak but has red face and red borders around eyes.

PURPLE-EDGED COPPER

Palaeochrysophanus hippothoe   32–38mm

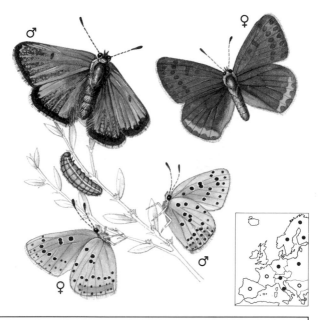

Fore wings of male red-gold with black borders, often purple along the leading edge; hind wings generally darker and shot with purple. Fore wings of female generally darker with dark brown spots and border, hind wings dark with orange marginal band.

Found in bogs and damp meadows, near streams and springs across much of central and northern Europe, from lowlands to 1500m. Absent from much of northern and western France, southern Spain and Britain.

Caterpillar short and stout, deep green with short hairs, a dark line along its back and two paler lines along each side. It feeds on sorrel and bistort.

Violet Copper flies in wet meadows in northern Europe. Males have wings suffused with purple, females have black-marked, orange fore wings, dark grey hind wings.

May–July

Wings of male dark grey-brown with black spots and a row of orange crescents. Fore wings of female orange with black spots and border, hind wings dark brown with an orange band on the margin enclosing black spots. Hind wings have a small lobe at the rear.

Found in lowland meadows and grassland across central and southern Europe, north to Germany and Poland. Absent from much of Spain (and then present in mountain meadows), northern Europe and Britain.

Caterpillar short and stout, bright green with tiny white spots, sometimes with red-brown stripes on back and sides. It may look like a small bulge in a leaf. It feeds on docks and sorrels.

Female **Purple-edged Copper** similar but orange marginal band does not enclose black spots. **Scarce Copper** female has orange hind wings, heavily blotched with black.

April–May & Aug–Sept

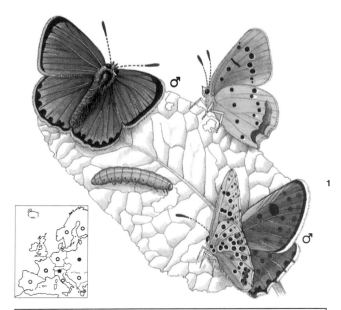

1

Wings of male brilliant copper with black borders. Wings of female also brilliant copper with many black spots. Underside of wings of both sexes yellow-red, with black spots on both wings and white spots on hind wings.

Found in damp meadows from lowlands to 2000m in the south of its range. Across much of Europe from Spain to the Balkans and north to Scandinavia. Absent from lowlands of France, Belgium and the Netherlands and absent from Britain.

Caterpillar short and stout, dark green with a pale stripe along its back and each side, covered with pale hairs. It feeds on docks.

Purple-shot Copper (1) flies in meadows across much of Europe but not in Britain. Male has reddish-orange wings suffused with purple, female has dark brown wings, both with black spots.

July–August

Wings of male copper-orange with black borders and one or two black spots. Fore wings of female with many black spots, hind wings blackish with orange marginal band. Underside of fore wing orange with grey marginal band, hind wing grey with orange marginal band, both with white-ringed black spots.

Found locally across much of Europe, in wet meadows, marshes and fens; becoming rare due to land drainage. Became extinct in Britain in the 1850s where it lived in the eastern fenland; reintroduced to Wood Walton Fen but only surviving with help.

Caterpillar bright green with darker stripes on the side, slug-like in shape with a flattened underside. It feeds on the undersides of the leaves of water dock, chewing large holes in the leaves.

Scarce Copper has yellow-red undersides with black spots on both wings and white spots on hind wings. **Purple-edged Copper** females have dark fore wings as well as hind wings.

Fore wings bright orange-copper with black spots and black border; hind wings bronze-black with irregular orange stripe on rear margin. Underside of fore wing pale orange with white-ringed black spots, of hind wing pale grey with black spots and an irregular orange stripe at the rear.

Found in open grassland and waste places, on downs, heaths and dunes, roadside verges, anywhere its caterpillar foodplant occurs. Throughout Europe and the British Isles from lowlands to 2000m.

Caterpillar shaped like a dark green woodlouse, sometimes with pink stripes. It feeds on the undersides of the leaves of sorrel and sheep's sorrel, forming characteristic grooves.

There are several varieties of this butterfly. One of the most common is especially frequent in Scotland and northern Europe; it has a row of blue spots on the hind wing.

Feb–Oct

♀

Wings dark brown with transverse rows of irregular orange spots towards the edges of the wings, larger on the fore wings and also larger in female. Underside of fore wing with similar markings, of hind wings brown with two transverse rows of white spots.

Found in rides and clearings in woods, in calcareous grassland and meadows, usually in lowland areas. In small local colonies across central and southern Europe from Spain to the Balkans, north to England and southern Sweden.

Caterpillar hairy, short and stout with an arched back. Pale brown, lighter on the back, with a line of dark dashes along each flank. Feeds on primroses in woodland and cowslips in grassland.

More closely related to blues and coppers than to other butterflies, in spite of its resemblance to a small fritillary.

May–June (N) & Aug (S)

MARSH FRITILLARY

Eurodryas aurinia 30–46mm

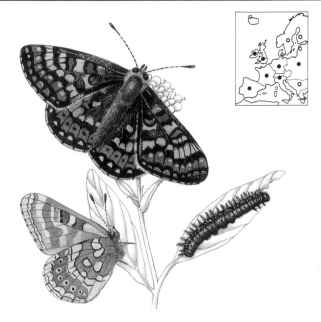

Wings patterned in orange, yellow and dark brown with a row of black spots towards edge of hind wing. Underside of fore wings pale orange and yellow, with two orange-red patches; hind wings orange, with four pale spots near base, otherwise pattern like upper side.

Found in small colonies in wet grassland, moors and mountain meadows from lowlands to 1500m. Much of the British Isles and Europe, north to southern Sweden. Absent from Norway, southern Italy and Greece.

Caterpillar black with bands of white spots on the back and sides, and with black, bristly spines. Feeds on devil's-bit scabious in Britain, on this and field scabious and plantain on the continent.

Most other fritillaries with similar chequered wings lack the row of black spots. Spanish Fritillary does have black spots but is confined to hills and mountains of southern Spain.

Wings with a variable, chequered pattern of dark brown and orange, and white fringes. Underside of fore wings pale orange, yellow crescents at the margin edged with black veins. Underside of hind wings orange with two pale yellow bands and various spots, the bands and spots edged with black.

Found in meadows and grassland, woodland clearings and heathland, up to 1500m, throughout much of Europe. Formerly widespread in southern Britain but now restricted to a few colonies in Kent and the southwest.

Caterpillar black with white speckles, underside and prolegs grey-green; with fleshy orange spines and black bristles. Feeds mainly on cow-wheat and ribwort, but also on foxglove and speedwells.

Meadow Fritillary flies in hills and mountains of France and Spain; its orange-red wings have light, regular black markings. Provençal Fritillary is orange-yellow with light markings.

Wings dark brown with orange squares and spots mainly on fore wings. Underside of fore wings orange with rows of paler spots; of hind wings paler orange, with a double row of yellow and white spots in the middle, a row of yellow spots on the margin, and a row of small black and white spots between the two.

Found in damp lowland and mountain meadows up to 1800m. Widespread but local from northern Spain and southern France eastwards to the Balkans and north to Scandinavia and Finland. Absent from Britain, southern Italy, southern Spain and Greece.

Caterpillar grey-brown with orange spines and a dark head. Feeds on plantains, speedwells and cow-wheats.

Heath Fritillary is generally less dark and lacks the row of black and white spots on the underside of the hind wing; the two species are very similar however and may be confused.

May–July

Wings of male tawny red with black markings varying from spots to a heavy network, but often with an unspotted band inside the black-marked borders. Of female variably flushed with grey. Underside of fore wings paler orange with yellow tips; of hind wings pale yellow with orange bands & black spots.

Found in woodland clearings, lowland and mountain meadows up to 1500m throughout much of Europe, from the Mediterranean to the Baltic Sea. Absent from Britain, Holland, northern Germany, Finland and Scandinavia.

Caterpillar whitish with black lines running along the body and two rows of orange blotches along the back, each one around an orange spine; other spines whitish. Feeds on plantains, toadflax and speedwells.

Lesser Spotted Fritillary flies in rough grassy places in Spain and eastern Europe; it has triangular black spots on underside margin of hind wing (Spotted Fritillary spots usually round).

Wings orange-brown with a network of black lines and veins. Underside of fore wing pale orange with dim black pattern, and yellow wing tips crossed by black lines and spots; of hind wing pale straw yellow with orange bands and rows of black spots.

Found in flowery meadows from lowlands to over 1800m, throughout Europe from the south to southern Scandinavia and extreme southern Finland, but only in the Isle of Wight and Channel Islands in Britain. Absent from southern Spain.

Caterpillar black with vertical bands of white spots and short black spines on olive-green warts; head, legs and prolegs red. Feeds voraciously in groups within silken webs, usually on plantains, but also on hawkweeds and knapweeds.

Knapweed Fritillary is similar but has a well-defined orange band near the edge of the hind wings without black spots; it flies in meadows and slopes in central and southern Europe.

May–June & Aug–Sept (S); June–July (N)   65

Wings bright orange-brown with many series of black spots. Underside of fore wing paler with similar pattern; of hind wing dark red-brown and yellowish, with several silver spots near the base and in the centre, and a row of black-edged silver spots around the margin.

Usually found in woodland clearings and margins, sometimes in meadows, marshes and open moorland, from lowlands to 1800m. Across central Europe from Britain (but not Ireland) to Romania. Absent from S. Spain, much of Italy and Greece.

Caterpillar dark brown or black, speckled with white, with a broken white line along the back. Branched black spines have yellow bases and the two spines behind the head are longer and point forwards, like horns. Feeds on violets.

The very similar **Pearl-bordered Fritillary** has different undersides to its hind wings, with one silver spot in the centre and no black edge to its marginal silver spots.

Wings bright orange-brown with many series of black spots, females larger and darker than males with heavier spots. Underside of fore wing paler with similar pattern; of hind wing pale greenish-yellow with reddish blotches, a single silver spot in the centre and a row of silver spots around the margin.

Found in open damp woods, meadows and heaths, from lowlands to 1800m. Throughout much of Europe except for southern Spain. More common in the west of Britain than the east. Only in the Burren in Ireland.

Caterpillar black with a broken white line along the back and a row of white spots along each side; branched spines may be black or yellow. Feeds on violets.

The very similar **Small Pearl-bordered Fritillary** has different undersides to its hind wings, with several silver spots in the centre and black-edged silver spots on the margin.

April–May & July–Aug (S); May–June (N)   67

Fore wings concave. Wings orange-brown with rows of black spots. Underside of fore wings paler orange-brown with similar pattern of black spots; of hind wings even paler with large silver spots near base, a line of smaller, black-ringed silver spots, and another line of large silver spots around margins.

Found in dry open grassland, heaths and meadows from sea-level to over 2000m. Resident in southern Europe, commonly migrating north each year to reach the southern half of Scandinavia and Finland. Occasionally crossing into S. England.

Caterpillar black with bristly spines, speckled with white and with a broken yellowish stripe along each side. Feeds on violets.

Other fritillaries have smaller silver spots on the undersides, or lack silver spots altogether.

Quite large fritillary. Wings bright orange-brown, with black spots and veins; males have two raised narrow veins on the fore wings. Underside of hind wings greenish with silver or yellowish spots; one small spot near the base of the hind wing often has a tiny black spot in its centre.

Found in woodland clearings, meadows and pastures, often in the mountains (up to 2500m). Across Europe from central Spain and France to the Balkans and Greece, north to Scandinavia and Finland. Absent from Britain.

Caterpillar red-brown, mottled with black and with long pinkish, black-barbed spines. Square black spots on the back are divided by a white line running along the back and bordered by white spots. Head shaggy and yellow-brown. Feeds on violets.

High Brown Fritillary is generally larger; it does not have a white spot with a tiny black mark in it on the underside of the hind wing.

June–July   69

Large fritillary. Wings bright orange-brown with black spots and veins; in males two of the veins on fore wings are raised. Underside of fore wings pale orange-brown with greenish tips, of hind wings greenish near the base, with many silver or yellowish spots and a row of reddish, silver-centred spots.

Found in wide woodland rides and clearings, rough grassland and heaths, especially in hills and mountains. Across the whole of Europe except for northern Scandinavia and northern Finland. Only found rarely in the southern half of Britain.

Caterpillar dark brown, variably flecked with grey, and with a white stripe along the back running through triangular dark marks. Spines pale red brown or pink. Feeds on dog violets.

Niobe Fritillary is very similar. **Dark Green Fritillary** has no reddish silver-centred veins on underside of hind wing; fore wing has no raised veins.

DARK GREEN FRITILLARY

Mesoacidia aglaja   48–58mm

Large fritillary. Wings of male bright orange-brown with black marks and spots. Underside of fore wings pale orange-pink and of hind wings yellowish, overlaid with dull green and with large silver spots; there is a row of silver spots on the margin of both wings. Female similar but slightly paler with larger black spots.

Found in grassy slopes, meadows, downs, heaths and dunes, less often in grassy woodland clearings. Attracted to thistles and other purple-flowered plants. Throughout Europe and the British Isles, from lowlands high into the mountains.

Caterpillar matt black with branched black spines, white speckles and a series of orange-red blotches along each side. Feeds on violets.

In the **High Brown Fritillary** there is a row of reddish, silver-centred spots on the underside of each hind wing; and males have two raised veins on the fore wings.

Large fritillary. Wings of male bright orange-brown with black marks and spots; underside of fore wings tawny orange with greenish tips and similar black pattern to upper side, of hind wings greenish grey with silver stripes. Wings of female duller and paler, often with heavier black markings.

Found in woodland rides and clearings, often around brambles, from lowlands to 1400m. Across Europe from Ireland and the southern half of Britain to the Balkans and Greece, north to southern Scandinavia and Finland. Absent from southern Spain.

Caterpillar has a dark brown back with two yellow stripes, mottled brown sides with darker lines, and black-tipped, red-brown spines; the first two spines are black and point forwards over the head. Feeds on violets.

The **Cardinal** is similar but its fore wing undersides are rosy red at the base, green at the tips, and its hind wing undersides are light green with silver streaks.

Cardinal (1)

Wingspan: 64–80mm. The largest European fritillary. Wings orange-brown with black spots & marks. Male somewhat, female more heavily flushed with green-grey. Female larger. Underside of fore wings rose-red at base, green at tips; of hind wing green, with narrow silver stripes more obvious in female. Found in woods & meadows to 2000m, across S. Europe from Spain & S. France to the Balkans & Greece. Flies June–July. Caterpillar feeds on violets.

Lesser Marbled Fritillary (2)

Wingspan: 34–40mm. Wings orange-red with linear black markings & black borders. Flies in wet marshy meadows up to 1500m in C. & N. Europe, in June–July. Caterpillar feeds on meadowsweet, burnet & related plants. Marbled Fritillary is similar but larger (wingspan 42–52mm), with orange-red wings & black spots & marks. It flies in June–July in warm valleys in S. & E. Europe. Caterpillar feeds on brambles & violets.

Scarce Fritillary (2)
Wingspan: 42–50mm. Wings
banded & spotted in dark
brown, orange-red & pale
yellow; with two large, black-
edged orange-red spots near top
middle of fore wing, separated
by a yellow space, & a series of
small white spots on hind
wings. Found locally, often in
valleys or near streams,
scattered across Europe, east,
northeast & southeast of Paris.
Flies May–June. Caterpillars
hibernate in silken webs on
trees, then disperse to feed on
plantains, speedwells & other
plants.

Cranberry Fritillary (1)
Wingspan: 32–42mm. Wings
bright tawny red with V-shaped
black marks in the middle of the
fore wing, & other distinct
zigzagging marks & spots on
both wings. Found in peat-bogs
from lowlands to mountains, in
N. Europe. Flies June–July.
Caterpillar feeds on cranberry.
The similar Shepherd's
Fritillary flies high in the
mountains of C. & S. Europe. It
has less definite, less zigzagging
markings.

74

Bog Fritillary (1)
Wingspan: 40–46mm. Wings
tawny yellow with dark zigzag
markings & spots. Underside of
hind wing yellow & orange,
with bands of large, gleaming
yellow or white spots in the
middle & on the margin, & a
row of black-edged, small white
spots near the edge. Found in
marshes, wet meadows & bogs,
scattered very locally in N. & C.
Europe. Flies June–July.
Caterpillar feeds on bistort,
violets & cranberry.

Violet Fritillary (2)
Wingspan: 32–34mm. Wings
tawny orange with clear black
marks & spots. Underside of
hind wing suffused with purple,
with a band of clear white spots
across the middle, & a row of
prominent black, white-centred
spots towards the margin.
Found in open woods,
heathland and hills up to 900m,
all across C. Europe from
France & Belgium eastward, &
north to Scandinavia. Flies
Apr–Sept. Caterpillar feeds on
violets & brambles.

Spring form has red-brown wings with black marks and spots; undersides also red-brown with white veins and cross-lines, and a broad, broken white band, often across both wings. Late summer form black with a broken, white or pale yellow band across both wings; underside similar to spring form.

Found in woodland rides and clearings, around woodland margins and riversides. Mainly in lowland areas across central Europe from western France eastwards to Romania, and in N. Spain. Absent from the south and north, and from Britain.

Caterpillar black with white speckles, yellow or black spines and yellow prolegs. Feeds in groups on stinging nettles.

Spring form is like a small fritillary. Late summer form is like a small **White Admiral**.

Wings tawny-orange to pinkish buff, with black, white-spotted tips to fore wings, and rows of black spots on hind wings. One blue spot occurs at inside rear edge of hind wing. Underside of fore wing pink and black with white spots; hind wing variegated in pale browns, black and white, with a row of eye-spots.

Resident in Africa, migrating north each year to reach almost all Europe, commonly in Britain and southern Scandinavia. Found in many habitats, often in open countryside or waste land, attracted by flowers. Does not overwinter in Europe.

Caterpillar black, speckled with tiny white spots and with many black or yellowish spines; it has a discontinuous yellow line along each side. Feeds mainly on thistles, also on nettles or mallows, forming silken webs on the underside of the leaves.

Tortoiseshells do not have black, white-spotted wing tips, their wings lack the pinkish tinge and they have a row of blue spots on their hind wings.

April–Oct (N); most of year (S)

PEACOCK
54–60mm

Inachis io

Wings brownish-red with a single large 'peacock' eyespot, ringed with yellow and black, on each wing. Underside almost black, metallic, crossed by fine dark lines.

Mobile butterflies found in many habitats, rural and urban, attracted by flowers. Widespread and often common throughout much of Europe and Britain, becoming more rare in Scotland and absent from northern Scandinavia and much of Finland.

Caterpillar velvety black, covered with black spines, speckled with white spots. Prolegs yellow-brown. Feeds on stinging nettles, at first in groups in silken webs, later leaving the webs and dispersing.

No similar butterfly.

Wings tawny orange with dark markings and irregular, scalloped margins. Undersides variegated dark brown and yellow brown, with a silver 'comma' mark on the hind wing. Some individuals in the summer have less deeply scalloped wing margins and brighter, paler wings, with paler undersides.

Found in open countryside, in gardens, around woodland margins from lowlands to 1800m throughout much of Europe, north to Sweden, Finland, the southern half of England and Wales. Also migrating into Norway.

Caterpillar black with orange-brown bands on its sides and a large white patch on its back; it resembles a bird dropping. Spines light orange-brown, but white on white patch. Feeds singly on the undersides of stinging nettle leaves.

Southern Comma is found in hot dry places across southern Europe; it has yellow-brown wings with small black spots and a small 'Y' mark on the underside of the hind wing.

March–April & June–August   79

Wings orange-red, darker towards base; large black blotches on fore wings separated by pale yellow spaces with a white space towards the tip. There are blue crescents around margins of both wings. Underside dark grey near base and yellow-brown towards margins, markings similar to those on upper surface.

Highly mobile, migrant butterflies which may be seen in any habitat, rural or urban, attracted by flowers. Common throughout Europe and Britain from sea-level to over 2000m.

Caterpillar has many spines; it has a black back with tiny white spots, two discontinuous yellow bands along the sides, and may be black or yellow on the underside. Feeds on stinging nettles, at first in groups in silken webs, later singly.

Large Tortoiseshell is larger, with darker yellow spaces between the black marks on the fore wings, with no white space near the fore wing tip.

March–Oct

Wings with ragged margins, orange-brown with several black blotches on fore wings separated by yellow spaces; black marginal borders enclose orange-brown and blue crescents (blue ones usually only on hind wings). Underside dark brown near base, paler and yellow-brown towards edges. Legs dark brown.

Found in open woods and around woodland margins throughout much of continental Europe, migrating into Scandinavia and southern Finland each year. In Britain it is found mainly in southern England and is absent from Ireland.

Caterpillar black with white speckles, orange lines along back and sides, and many sharp, forked, yellowish spines. Feeds in groups, on leaves of elms and willows, at first in conspicuous silken webs, later leaving the webs but staying in groups.

Scarce Tortoiseshell is similar but has pale brown or buff legs; it flies in woods in eastern Europe. **Small Tortoiseshell** has white, not yellow, space near tip of fore wings.

June–Sept & April–May   81

Wings dark purple-brown with a row of bright blue spots near the edges and ragged yellow margins. Underside mottled grey with a yellowish border.

Found in light woodland and open countryside, often in hills and mountains. Scattered throughout much of continental Europe, migrating into Scandinavia and Finland each year but a rare migrant in Britain. Absent from most of Spain except the north.

Caterpillar black with many tiny white spots and red blotches along its sides; it has many black spines and bristles. Feeds in groups in a silken web at first, later in groups or alone, on willows, birch and elm.

No similar butterfly.

Wings black with red stripe across fore wings and along rear of hind wings (containing black spots on hind wings), white spots on fore wing tips and a broken white line around both wings. Underside of fore wing blackish, brown and white on tips with a red bar across; of hind wings mottled brown, black and blue.

Found in many urban and rural habitats; attracted to flowers, and to fallen fruits in late summer. Most of Europe but only overwintering south of the Alps, migrating north in large numbers each year, to northern Britain and Scandinavia.

Caterpillar usually black with yellow spots along the sides and black spines; less often grey-green or yellowish with pale spines. Feeds on stinging nettles, singly at first in silken webs, later within curled leaves.

No other European butterfly is quite like this one.

May–Oct

Wings brown-black with a wide band of white spots, and other white spots towards the tip of the fore wing; and with three rows of black spots towards the edges of both wings. Underside tawny orange, grey near inner edge of hind wings, and with similar markings to upper side.

Found in rides and clearings in damp woods from lowlands to 900m. Across central Europe from northern Spain, France and southern Britain to Romania and north to southern Sweden. Absent from southeastern France, southern Italy and Greece.

Caterpillar green with a purplish underside and two rows of brown spines along its back. Feeds on honeysuckle.

Southern White Admiral has blue-edged dark spots near wing margins; found in woods in southern Europe. Common Glider has three bands of white spots; found in woods in E. Europe.

June–July

Wings dark brown with bands of white spots, often indistinct in male, larger and better defined in female, and orange and black spots around the margins, larger on hind wings. Underside orange with similar markings in blue-grey or white and a double row of black spots near the edges of the hind wings.

Found in damp open woods and forests, usually among the tree tops. From sea-level to 1000m, from southeastern France eastwards, migrating to Scandinavia and Finland some years. Absent from western France, Spain, Portugal and Britain.

Caterpillar green with a yellowish band along its sides, and purple-brown spots along its back and beneath the band. It has two rows of spiny projections along its back, the first two long and pointing forward. Feeds on aspen and other poplars.

White Admiral has much darker wings and no orange spots around the margin. **Purple Emperors** have wings flushed with purple and one or more solitary dark spots.

June–July

Wings of male almost black flushed with iridescent purple; three interrupted lines of white spots on fore wing, one on hind wing with a single dark spot. Female paler with no purple sheen and broader creamy white spots. Undersides brown and grey with similar markings plus an extra dark spot on fore wing.

Found in old deciduous woodland and around old hedgerows. Mainly in lowlands, across central Europe from northern Spain and southern Britain eastward; absent from much of southern Europe (including south of France and Italy), and Scandinavia.

Caterpillar shaped like a woodlouse with a pointed tail. It is green and granular in appearance with diagonal yellow lines; its head has two pink-tipped, forward-pointing horns. Feeds on leaves of goat willow, grey and crack willows.

Lesser Purple Emperor has dark, orange-ringed spots on the fore wings. **Admirals** have bands of white spots but no single dark spots and their wings are not flushed with purple.

Similar to Purple Emperor but with a large, dark, orange-ringed spot on each fore wing. Underside may be suffused with brown all over.

Found in woodland, often in damp places or near streams, across central Europe from France to Romania, north to Poland in the east. Absent from northwest including Britain, Holland and northwest Germany. Also absent from southern Italy & Greece.

Caterpillar shaped like woodlouse, tapering towards the pointed tail. It is green with diagonal red and yellow stripes and with two long forward-pointing, brown-tipped horns on its head. Feeds on poplar, aspen and willows.

Purple Emperor lacks the dark, orange-ringed spots on the fore wings. **Admirals** have no single ringed spots and their wings are not flushed with purple.

May–June & Aug–Sept   87

Wings rich brown with wide yellow-brown margins, the hind wings with black borders outside the yellow margins and blue spots inside, also with two tails. Underside brown with white-ringed dark spots and bands of white and yellow towards the edges.

Found locally in dry hills up to 800m, around the Mediterranean coastline from France to Greece. Absent from Spain and Portugal and from the Adriatic coast.

Caterpillar green and covered with many tiny white dots; it has two dark-ringed, blue-centred yellow spots on its back and a large head with four backward-pointing prongs tipped with red. Feeds on leaves of strawberry trees.

No similar species.

Wings of male black with creamy white markings, consisting of an irregular band of blotches across the centre of both wings, with spots on either side. Underside with similar pattern but black areas flushed with white. Female similar but markings larger and whiter; underside of hind wing flushed with yellow.

Found in grassland and on downs, also on roadside verges and around woodland margins, from sea-level to 1500m. Throughout much of Europe from the Mediterranean to the Baltic coast, also in southern England and Wales. Absent from Scandinavia.

Caterpillar spindle-shaped, tapering at the tail to two reddish points; either light brown or yellow-green with darker and paler stripes along back and sides. Feeds on grasses, probably mainly fescues.

Several other Marbled Whites fly in southern Europe, three in Spain. In general their wings have much more extensive white markings, with the black areas much reduced and more delicate.

June–July   89

Wings black with a wide broken band of white across both wings and a single black spot on fore wing. Hind wings have scalloped margins. Underside similar in pattern but dark area mottled.

Found in open deciduous woodland, especially oak woods, often sitting on tree trunks, from lowlands to about 1400m. Across southern and central Europe from Portugal and France east to Czechoslovakia and Greece.

Caterpillar tapering from its striped head to the two points on its tail; it is very light brown on the back and sides, with dark brown stripes and a yellow-brown stripe on each side, and dark brown beneath. Feeds on brome and rye grasses.

No similar species.

Wings dark grey-brown, with broad yellow-white bands near
margins and two eye-spots on fore wing, one on hind wing; band
and spots more distinct in female. Hind wings have scalloped
margins. Underside of fore wing has similar pattern, hind wing
banded in mottled grey and white.

Found in open woods and woodland margins, often resting on
tree trunks with wings open; from lowlands to 1000m. Scattered
locally across central and southern Europe, from northern Spain
and southern France to southern Poland and Greece.

Caterpillar tapering from head to two points at the tail; pale
brown in colour with darker brown lines along back and sides.
Feeds on soft grasses, particularly on bromes and fescues.

Rock Grayling (1) is similar but smaller (wingspan 56–66mm); it
is found from Spain across central Europe but generally flies in
the mountains, in rough places up to 1500m or more.

July–August   91

Wings brown with variable yellowish bands near margins (larger in female), containing two white-centred, black spots on fore wing, one on hind wing. Hind wings scalloped on margins. Underside of fore wing tawny orange and brown, hind wing marbled brown, grey and black, both with spots as upper side.

Found in sheltered sunny places, in heaths and rough hillsides, coastal cliffs and dunes, dry woods and downs, from lowlands to 1500m. Throughout Europe north to southern Scandinavia and Finland. Mostly around the coasts in Britain and Ireland.

Caterpillar cigar-shaped, tapering to two points at the tail; head and body pale yellow-brown with darker brown stripes. Feeds on grasses by night, hiding by day.

Southern Grayling is almost indistinguishable but only found in Mediterranean islands and Greece. **False Grayling** has only one black spot on the fore wing, Baltic Grayling has several.

May–August

Wings dark grey-brown, paler towards margin with two black and two white spots on fore wing, one black spot on hind wing. In female black spots usually white-centred. Underside of fore wing similar to upper side, hind wing mottled in browns with sinuous black line across middle. Hind wing has scalloped edge.

Found in open woodland, scrub and heathland, often in hills. Scattered across central and southern Europe, from Portugal and France to Poland, becoming rare in many places.

Caterpillar tapers from head to the two points on the tail; it is pale brown in colour with darker brown lines along back and sides. Feeds on grasses, especially barren brome.

Striped Grayling has similar upper surface, but its hind wing underside has striking zig-zag pattern of dark lines; it flies in rocky places among trees in southern France and Iberia.

July–Sept   93

Wings brown with a variable orange band across both wings and a single dark spot on both wings. Underside of fore wing mostly orange with a single dark spot, of hind wing mottled dark brown with white band towards margin. Hind wings have scalloped margins. Female larger than male, with wider orange bands.

Found in heaths and grassy limestone places, up to 1200m. Widely distributed but local in southern Europe, from Portugal and France to eastern Europe and the Balkans.

Caterpillar tapering from its striped head to the two points on its tail; it is yellow-brown or grey, with dark brown stripes. Feeds on grasses, particularly on fescues.

Baltic Grayling has dark brown wings with a band of orange patches on both wings, some with black spots. It is one of several northern graylings found in Scandinavia and Finland.

July–August

Wings dark brown to almost black, female paler than male; male with or without, and female with, more or less dim eyespots on both wings. Undersides of both sexes paler and may be flushed with gold, with two conspicuous white-centred, yellow-ringed eyespots on each fore wing, five on hind wing.

Found in damp meadows, open woods, hedges and woodland margins, from lowlands to 1500m. Most of Europe and the British Isles, from northern Spain to southern Scotland, S. Scandinavia & Finland. Absent from S. Italy & most of Greece.

Caterpillar tapering towards the two points of the tail; yellowish and covered with dark bristles, with a white line along the back and several dark lines along the sides. Feeds on grasses, especially on tufted hair-grass or creeping bent.

False Ringlet is smaller, with underside eyespots on hind wing arranged four and one (not three and two as in Ringlet); it flies in wet meadows in parts of southern central Europe.

June–August   95

Wings of male dark brown, generally with two or three large and two small eyespots on fore wing, four on hind wing, all with orange-yellow circles around. Underside paler, uniform brown with similar eyespots. Female larger and paler, orange-yellow circles more extensive and more or less touching.

Found in damp meadows, moors and damp woods in lowlands in the north of its range, in damp mountain meadows in the south. From central France and Germany east to Poland, southeast to Greece. Absent from Spain, the Pyrenees and SW. Alps.

Caterpillar tapering from head to the two points at the tail, green or brown with a black band along the back and pale stripes along the sides. Feeds on grasses, especially crab grass and wood millet.

One of many ringlets in Europe, most mountain species. Mountain Ringlet flies in southern Europe, Scotland and the Lake District; it is brown with red bands and black spots.

May–July

ARRAN BROWN

Erebia ligea 48–54mm

1

Wings of male black with wide red band on both wings, three or four white-centred eyespots on fore wing, three on hind wing. Underside of fore wing similar to upper side of hind wing, banded in light and dark brown, with an irregular white streak. Female similar but dark brown with orange-red band.

Found in meadows and woods in hilly country, up to 1500m, through the Alps and Carpathians to the Balkans and Greece. Also in lowland areas of Scandinavia and Finland. Reported in Arran and the Scottish Highlands.

Caterpillar tapering from its head to the two points on its tail, pale brown or yellowish with a dark line running down its back and a broad white stripe on each side. Takes two years before it pupates. Feeds on crab grass and wood millet.

Scotch Argus (1) flies in meadows and woods, in hills of central Europe, Scotland and Cumbria. Male black, female dark brown, both with red bands and three eyespots on each wing.

July–August

MEADOW BROWN
40–58mm

Maniola jurtina

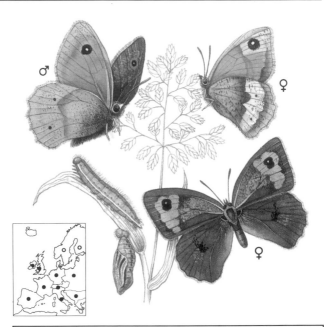

Wings of male dark brown with white-centred eyespot on fore wing. Underside of fore wing flushed with orange; of hind wing dark at base, paler and yellower towards margin with two small black spots. Female paler with orange area on both wings; underside of fore wing orange, hind wing often brightly banded.

Found in grassy places, meadows, roadside verges, grassy woodland rides and clearings, from sea-level to about 1800m. Throughout the British Isles and much of Europe, north to southern Scandinavia and Finland.

Caterpillar tapering from head towards the two white points of the tail; yellow-green on the back and darker green beneath, with a white line along each side and covered with long whitish hairs. Feeds on grasses, especially meadow grasses.

A very variable species. Males may have a flush of orange beneath the eyespot on fore wings. Particularly brightly coloured males are found in western Scotland.

June–Sept

Fore wings grey-brown, males slightly flushed with orange, a narrow dark streak across the middle and a single black spot; females heavily flushed with orange and two black spots. Hind wings of both grey-brown with a scalloped margin. Undersides similar but with more orange and black spots white-centred.

Found in dry rocky places, mainly in lowland areas. Central and southern Europe from the Mediterranean to Finland, but absent from most of France, the Netherlands, Scandinavia and Britain.

Caterpillar tapering towards the two points of the tail. It is bright green with two stripes on each side in differing shades of yellow. Its head is green with a white-edged black stripe at the back. Feeds on grasses, especially meadow grasses.

The one black spot on the fore wing of the **Meadow Brown** is white-centred on both sides of the wing.

July–August

Wings of male mid to dark brown, female light to mid brown, both with yellow-ringed spots on both wings. Underside of both sexes variably banded, grey near the margin and dark brown near the base with an irregular white streak across the centre; fore wing has single eyespot and hind wing has row of eyespots.

Found in marshes and wet meadows, peat bogs and rough wet moorlands, often among cotton grass, from lowlands to 600m. Central and northern Europe, from France eastward and north across much of Scandinavia; northern half of the British Isles.

Caterpillar tapering towards the two pink points of the tail; green with a dark line along the back and several yellow or white lines along the sides. Feeds on white beak-sedge and probably on cotton grass.

A common northern form is yellow-brown flushed with grey, and often lacks eyespots. **Chestnut Heath** (1) flies in grassy places, locally across Europe from northern Spain to Finland.

June–July

Wings bright yellow-brown with narrow grey borders and a small grey spot on each fore wing. Underside of fore wing orange near base, paler towards margin with a large, yellow-ringed eyespot; of hind wing olive-brown near base, a pale band across the centre, and grey towards margin with several eyespots.

Found in grassy places from sea level to 1800m. Common throughout the British Isles and Europe except the far north of Scandinavia.

Caterpillar tapers towards the two pink points of the tail; it is green with whitish green lines along the body. Feeds on various grasses, including meadow grasses and fescues.

Large Heath is larger and has no grey wing borders.

May–Sept   101

Fore wing orange with wide dark border; hind wing dark with a
trace of orange at rear, often with one or two eyespots.
Underside orange-brown, with a metallic border on hind wing,
sometimes on fore wing; hind wing crossed by an irregular pale
band and with several yellow-ringed, white-centred eyespots.

Found in open grassy woodland and around grassy slopes, often
in hills, from lowlands to 1200m. Northern Portugal and Spain
across Europe to Poland, southern Scandinavia and Greece.
Absent from Britain.

Caterpillar tapering to the two red-marked points of its tail;
green with a dark line along its back and yellow lines along each
side. Feeds on grasses, especially on melick.

Darwin's Heath and Alpine Heath are similar but smaller; they
are found only in high alpine meadows in the Alps and
Dolomites.

GATEKEEPER

Pyronia tithonus

34–38mm

Wings dark brown, with large orange patch on fore wing, smaller one on hind wing; and a single eyespot on each wing, the one on fore wing larger and with two white spots. Female has larger, brighter patches than male. Underside of hind wing (in both sexes) banded in brown and yellow, with small eyespots.

Found around brambles in hedgerows, woodland clearings and lanes, in lowland areas throughout much of Europe, north to Germany and Poland. Absent from Scandinavia and southern Italy. Also found in England, Wales and the far south of Ireland.

Caterpillar tapering towards the two points of the tail, yellow-white with darker speckles and many short whitish hairs; there is a dark line along the back and paler lines along the sides. Feeds on a variety of grasses, often on fescues and bents.

Southern Gatekeeper has no eyespots on underside of hind wing and male has dark markings on fore wing. It flies in hot dry bushy places from Portugal across southern Europe to Greece.

July–August

Fore wing orange-brown with brown borders, a network of brown veins and an eyespot; hind wing brown with orange patches and white-centred eyespots. Underside of fore wing similar to but paler than upper side; of hind wing banded and mottled in browns with a row of brown, black-centred eyespots.

Found in dry open grassland, roadsides and waste places, gardens and fields, heaths and cliffs, woodland clearings and hedgerows, from sea level to 1500m. Throughout Europe, north to southern Scandinavia. Also in England, Wales and Ireland.

Caterpillar tapering towards the two points of the tail; blue-green, covered with whitish hairs, and with yellow-white lines along back and sides. Feeds on a variety of grasses.

Large Wall Brown and Northern Wall Brown have much less orange on their wings, and although they have dark veins, their wings do not appear to be latticed.

LARGE WALL BROWN

Lasiommata maera   44–56mm

Fore wings brown with dark veins and a white-centred black eyespot (sometimes with two white spots) in an orange patch; hind wing with two or three white-centred eyespots in orange rings. Underside of fore wing similar but brighter, of hind wing mottled brown with a row of brown-ringed eyespots.

Found in rocky places, woodland clearings and margins, often on hillside slopes, from lowlands to mountains, up to 1800m. Common throughout most of Europe, but absent from Britain and parts of northern Scandinavia.

Caterpillar tapering towards the two points of the tail; pale green with a dark brown back stripe, two yellow stripes on each side, and a dark green stripe beneath the lower yellow one. Feeds on grasses, including wood barley and meadow grasses.

Northern Wall Brown is smaller, with dark cross-lines on fore wing and a wavy transverse line on hind wing. It flies in coniferous woods in southern Europe, Scandinavia and Finland.

May–June & Aug–Sept (S); June–July (N)   105

Wings grey-brown with pale yellow or orange patches, more on
fore wings; one eyespot on fore wing, three on hind wing in
orange or yellow patches. Underside of fore wing patterned in
orange and brown or yellow and brown; of hind wing banded in
shades of yellow-brown, tinged with green and with white spots.

Found in dappled sunlight and shade, in open woods, woodland
rides and clearings. Throughout Europe north to central
Scandinavia and Finland.

Caterpillar tapering towards the two points of the tail; bright
green with sparse whitish hairs, and with faint darker green and
yellowish lines running along body. Feeds on various grasses,
especially cock's-foot and couch grass.

Speckled Woods with orange patches on the wings are found in
southern Europe; those with pale yellow patches in eastern,
central and northern Europe and in Britain.

Black Satyr (2)
Wingspan 48–56mm. Wings of male black with one white-centred eyespot on fore wing; female similar but dark brown, often with second spot on fore wing. Underside of fore wing (of both sexes) paler with similar spot(s), hind wing banded & mottled in brown & white. Found in dry stony slopes in Iberia, S. France & N. Italy. Flies July–Aug. Great Sooty Satyr male similar, female pale brown, both with two white-centred black spots on fore wing. Found in rocky hills in S. Europe.

The Hermit (1)
Wingspan 42–68mm. Female larger than male. Wings dark brown with a broken white band on fore wing, continuous white band on hind wing. Two dark spots on fore wing. Underside of fore wing similar, of hind wing (male) banded & mottled in white & brown, (female) mottled brown. Found in dry stony places from lowlands to 2000m, C. & S. Europe. Flies May–Aug. Caterpillar feeds on grasses, especially blue moor grass.

OTHER BROWNS

The Dryad (1)
Wingspan 54–70mm. Wings of
male dark brown with two blue-
centred, black spots on fore
wing, sometimes one on hind
wing. Hind wings have
scalloped margins. Undersides
of wings similar but paler, hind
wing may be darker at the base,
lighter towards the margin.
Female larger & paler, both on
upper & lower sides, with larger
spots. Found in grassy slopes,
scrub & open woods, locally in
C. Europe. Flies July–Aug.
Caterpillar feeds on grasses.

Woodland Brown (2)
Wingspan: 50–56mm. Wings
light grey-brown, with a curved
row of large, yellow-ringed
eyespots towards the margin.
Underside similar but with
additional pale stripes either
side of the eyespots. The inside
stripe on the hind wing is white,
all others yellow. Found in open
woods from lowlands to 1000m,
locally across C. Europe from
France to southern Finland &
Bulgaria. Absent from Britain.
Flies in June–July. Caterpillar
feeds on grasses.

Wings tawny orange-brown with wide black margins spotted with white, and black veins. It has long fore wings. Undersides of wings similar in pattern but paler in colour.

Migrates far and wide in open country. Native to N. America but now established and resident in the Canary Islands, and occasional vagrants reach Spain, Portugal, France and England.

Caterpillar transversely striped in white, yellow and black, with a pair of filaments at the head and rear. Feeds on milkweeds in N. America, but on two native plants in the Canaries, one *Gossypium* and one *Euphorbia* species.

African Queen smaller, with black-bordered, light tawny-brown wings, white spots across fore wing tips and three black spots on hind wing; resident in Canaries, sometimes seen in Greece.

summer (N); all year (S)   109

Distinctive butterfly with long palps (mouthparts). Fore wings hooked but appear to be cut off at the tips, brown with orange patches and a single white spot. Hind wings similar but without the white spot.

Found in lowland areas in open countryside and open woods, around nettle-trees. Southern Europe from northern Spain and southern France to Greece and the Balkans, north to Hungary in eastern Europe; also migrating into the mountains in summer.

Caterpillar green with a white stripe along its back and a pink stripe on each side. Feeds on leaves of nettle-trees.

No similar species.

Wings bright tawny orange with veins and margins outlined in black; male has a conspicuous black sex brand on each fore wing. Underside of fore wing pale tawny orange, fading to yellow-grey at wing tips and dark at base; of hind wing more greenish orange. Antenna-tip orange beneath.

Found in grassy places, meadows, woodland rides, roadside verges, up to 1800m. Widespread throughout Europe, north to Denmark, Germany and Poland, and in England and Wales. Absent from Scandinavia, Scotland and Ireland.

Caterpillar has a large green head; its body is green with a dark line along the back and yellow-white stripes along the sides. It lives in a tube made of a rolled grass leaf; and feeds on grasses, including Yorkshire fog and Timothy.

Essex Skipper is very similar but its antenna-tips are black beneath. **Lulworth Skipper** has yellow spots on fore wings.

June–August   111

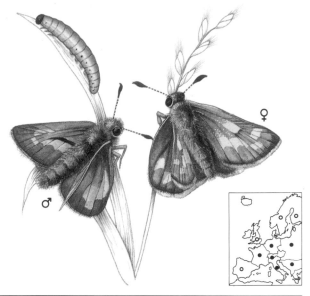

♀

♂

Wings of male patchy orange with wide, dark-brown margins and a broad black sex brand on fore wing. Wings of female dark brown, with several orange patches on fore wing, fewer on hind wing. Underside pale orange and greenish, same pattern as upper side and with a black streak beneath sex brand in male.

Found in grassy places, meadows, woodland margins, waste places and near the sea, to 1800m. Throughout much of Europe but absent from northern Scandinavia, Ireland and Scotland.

Caterpillar lives in a tube made from one or more rolled grass leaves, feeding on cock's-foot, false brome and other grasses. It has a large brown head and a blue-green body, with a dark line along the back and a yellow line along each side.

Silver-spotted Skipper is similar but for the silver spots that it has on the undersides of the wing.

Wings patchy orange with wide, dark brown margins and yellow spots near tips of fore wings; male has a broad black sex brand on each fore wing. Underside of fore wings yellow-brown near base, greenish with silvery spots towards the tips, of hind wings greenish with several silvery spots.

Found in grazed grassland, usually on chalk or limestone, from sea level to 2500m, in local colonies across much of Europe. Absent from much of the far north, southern Spain and Italy, and from Ireland. Now only in southern England in Britain.

Caterpillar grub-like, with a large black head and a dull olive-green, rough-skinned body. It lives in a tent-like shelter formed of grass leaves and feeds on grasses, usually sheep's fescue.

The otherwise similar **Large Skipper** lacks the silver spots.

July–August   113

Wings dark brown and chequered with many orange-yellow spots. Underside orange-yellow, often tinged with green on hind wings, both wings with bands of pale yellow spots in same pattern as on upper side.

Found in open woods up to 1500m, very locally across much of Europe, from France to the Balkans and northern Scandinavia. Absent from Denmark, southern Italy, most of Iberia. Probably extinct in England and only in western Inverness in Britain.

Caterpillar lives in a tube made from a rolled grass leaf. It is buff-coloured with darker pinkish brown and white lines and a large head. Feeds on grasses, including purple moor-grass and false brome.

Northern Chequered Skipper has yellow fore wings with brown spots, hind wings like Chequered Skipper. It flies in wooded valleys from northern Germany to Finland and Scandinavia.

June–July

Wings plain dark brown but for three or four yellow spots near tip of each fore wing. Fringes chequered. Underside of fore wing also brown with yellow markings around the tip; of hind wing yellow with twelve large, whitish, dark-ringed spots and a dark band along inner margin.

Found in damp meadows and bogs, woodland clearings and rides. Scattered in small colonies locally in northern Spain, western and northern France, in Switzerland and N. Italy; also in Jersey. More widely distributed in Europe east of Germany.

Caterpillar lives in a tube made from a rolled grass leaf. It has a large pale, brown-striped head and a grey-white body with a dark line along the back and a white line along each side. Feeds on grasses, including false brome and purple moor grass.

With its distinctive wings, this skipper is unlikely to be mistaken for any other.

June–August

Fore wings dark brown crossed by white-powdered bands and rows of white spots; hind wings dark brown with bands of white spots. Underside golden brown with bands of less distinct cream-coloured spots near the margins. Male has fold in fore wing.

Found in downs and heaths, cliffs and dunes, roadside verges, often on calcareous soils, from sea-level to 1800m. Across Europe, north to southern Scandinavia; also in England and Wales, parts of Ireland and on some Scottish coasts.

Caterpillar is quite stout but tapers towards head and tail. It has a purplish black head and grey-green body, covered with short white hairs. Found in a shelter of leaves on its foodplant, bird's-foot trefoil.

Only Inky Skipper, from the mountains of Greece and the Balkans, is similar and it lacks the white spots.

May–June (N); May–August (S)

Wings black, with irregular rows of distinct white spots and chequered black and white margins. Underside of fore wing grey-brown overlaid with white scales, of hind wing greenish or yellowish brown, both with white spots in a similar pattern to upper side; spots on hind wing larger than on upper side.

Found in flowery meadows and bogs, woodland rides and edges, from sea-level to 2000m across much of Europe, and in England and Wales. Absent from northern Scandinavia, Scotland and Ireland.

Caterpillar lives in a silk shelter beneath a leaf of its food plant, usually wild strawberry or one of the cinquefoils. It has a large black head and a yellow-green body, striped with darker brown and olive; it has many short pale hairs.

There are 13 similar related species in Europe, all difficult to tell apart.

April–June & July–August   117

A variable species and the smallest European skipper. Wings
dark brown to black with scattered white spots and a row of
white spots near each margin, or with scattered yellow spots.
Underside of fore wing dark grey, of hind wing brick red or red-
brown, both with curved bands of pale whitish spots.

Found in dry rough places from lowlands to mountains, up to
1500m. From Spain and Portugal locally through southern
Europe to southern Germany, Austria and southern Italy.

Caterpillar lives in a shelter of leaves woven together with silk. It
is short with a large head; its body is black with a yellowish
stripe along the back and it has many long white hairs. It feeds
on brambles, cinquefoils and burnet.

Hungarian Skipper is a related species, similar but for the olive-
green colour of the hind wing underside. It flies in rough ground
in eastern Europe, the Balkans and Greece.

Wings marbled brown, dark brown and grey, with glassy spots
on fore wings. Hind wings have scalloped margins. Undersides
paler brown with similar glassy spots on fore wing, and white or
yellow spots on hind wing.

Found around flowery banks, on hills and slopes up to 1500m.
Throughout central and southern Europe, north to central
France and Germany, east to the Ukraine.

Caterpillar lives in a shelter formed of leaves. It has a large black
head with orange spots around the neck; the body is greenish
grey speckled with black and white and with many short whitish
hairs. It feeds on mallow, marsh mallow and hibiscus.

Marbled Skipper has olive-brown wings marbled with olive
green and with white or glassy spots. It flies in dry chalky hills,
mainly in southern Europe, more rarely north of the Alps.

April–August   119

Essex Skipper (1)
Wingspan 24–28mm. Wings
tawny orange-brown with black
veins & margins; underside of
fore wing pale orange-brown
with yellow-grey wing tips and a
dark streak in centre, of hind
wing mainly yellow-grey. Male
has black sex-brand on fore
wing. Underside of antenna-tip
black. Found in meadows &
grassy hillsides across Europe,
north to southern Scandinavia;
also in southern England. Flies
June–Aug, often with the
similar **Small Skipper**.
Caterpillar feeds on various
grasses.

Lulworth Skipper (2)
Wingspan 22–26mm. Wings
dusky orange, fore wing with
one indistinct yellow spot near
centre & a curved series of
similar yellow spots towards
wing tip. Underside plain dusky
yellow. Male has black sex-
brand on fore wing. Scattered in
damp meadows & grassy places
across S. & C. Europe, only
near coast in Devon & Dorset in
Britain. Flies May–Aug.
Caterpillar feeds on brome-grass
& false brome-grass.

Large Grizzled Skipper (1)
Wingspan: 28–32mm. Wings dark grey-brown, with white spots on fore wing, large glassy mark & faint white spots on hind wing. Underside of hind wing olive-brown or green with large white marks. Found in flowery meadows in hills & mountains across S. & C. Europe, rare further north to southern Scandinavia; absent from Britain. Flies June–Aug. Caterpillar feeds on cinquefoils, rock rose & brambles. Similar Safflower Skipper is found in similar places in C. & S. Europe.

Olive Skipper (2)
Wingspan: 24–28mm. Wings dark grey-brown with variable white spots on fore wing (sometimes almost absent especially in female) & almost plain hind wings (spots if present very indistinct). Found in hills & mountains up to 2400m, across much of S. & C. Europe. Absent from northwest France, Holland & Britain. Flies June–Aug. Caterpillar feeds on lady's mantle & cinquefoils. One of several similar small skippers found in Europe.

121

Index and Checklist

All species in Roman type are illustrated.
Keep a record of your sightings by ticking the boxes.